GECKOS!

A MY INCREDIBLE WORLD PICTURE BOOK

MY INCREDIBLE WORLD

Copyright © 2023, My Incredible World

All rights reserved. This book or any portion thereof may not be reproduced or used in any manner whatsoever without the express written permission of the copyright holder.

www.myincredibleworld.com

Geckos are **reptiles**, which means they are cold-blooded animals.

Geckos are found in various parts of the world, including Asia, Africa, Australia, and the Americas.

There are over 1,500 different species of geckos, and they come in different shapes, sizes, and colors.

Geckos are known for their ability to climb walls and walk on ceilings due to their unique feet.

They have specialized toe pads covered in microscopic hairs called **setae**, which allow them to stick to surfaces.

The dwarf gecko is one of the smallest reptiles in the world!

Some species can change their colors to blend in with their surroundings.

Geckos communicate with each other through various vocalizations, including chirps, clicks, and squeaks.

They have a lifespan ranging from 10 to 25 years, depending on the species.

Geckos are mostly **insectivorous**, meaning they eat insects such as crickets, spiders, and moths.

They have long, sticky tongues that they use to catch their prey.

Some geckos can lose their tails when threatened by predators. Their tails can then regenerate over time!

They can shed their skin to allow for growth and to remove any parasites.

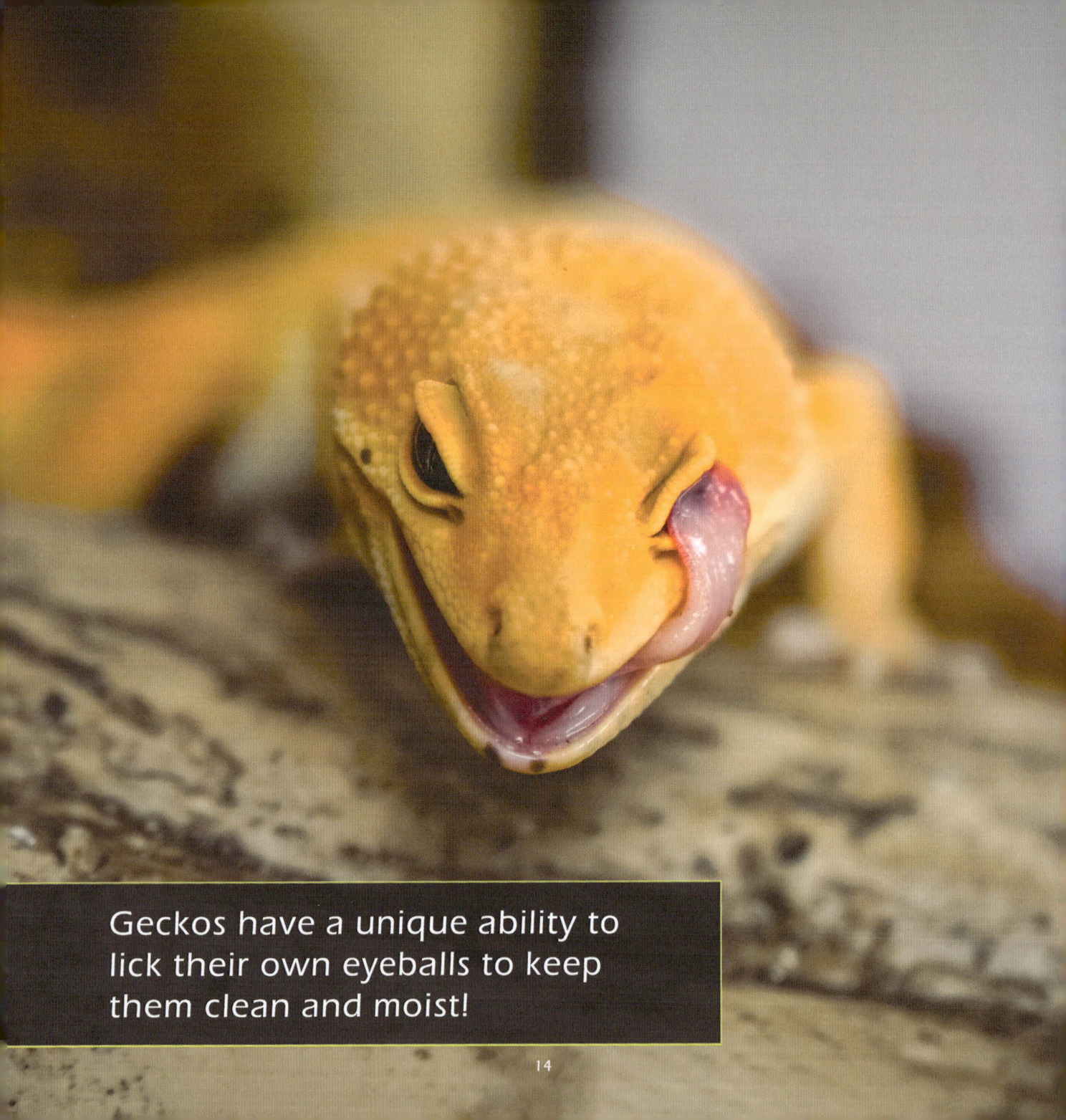

Geckos have a unique ability to lick their own eyeballs to keep them clean and moist!

They have a protective transparent membrane, called a **spectacle**, that helps cover and clean their eyes.

Geckos are mainly **oviparous**, which means they give birth by laying eggs.

Baby geckos, like all baby lizards, are called **hatchlings**.

Geckos have excellent eyesight and can see well even in low light conditions.

Some species are known for their ability to glide through the air using flaps of skin on their bodies!

Geckos have a strong jaw and sharp teeth to help them grip and chew their food.

Some species are known for their unique ability to walk on water.

Geckos are incredible!

Printed in Great Britain
by Amazon